THE WINNER'S WAY

**Celebrate Your Success
One Win at a Time**

A Gratitude Journal for Daily Triumphs

DR SCOTT ZARCINAS

This Winner's Journal belongs to

_____

THE WINNER'S WAY

**Celebrate Your Success
One Win at a Time**

A Gratitude Journal for Daily Triumphs

DR SCOTT ZARCINAS

DoctorZed
Publishing
www.doctorzed.com

Copyright © Scott Zarcinas 2024

All rights reserved. No part of this book may be used or reproduced by any means, graphic, electronic, or mechanical, including photocopying, recording, taping or by any information storage retrieval system without the written permission of the publisher except in the case of brief quotations embodied in critical articles and reviews.

Copies of this book can be ordered via the author's website at www.scottzarcinas.com, booksellers or by contacting:

DoctorZed Publishing
10 Vista Ave, Skye,
South Australia 5072
www.doctorzed.com

ISBN: 978-0-9756145-4-9 (hc)
ISBN: 978-0-9756145-5-6 (sc)
ISBN: 978-0-9756145-6-3 (e)

A CiP number is available at the National Library of Australia.

Because of the dynamic nature of the Internet, any web addresses or links contained in this book may have changed since publication and may no longer be valid. The views expressed in this work are solely those of the author and do not necessarily reflect the views of the publisher, and the publisher hereby disclaims any responsibility for them.

The author of this book does not dispense medical advice or prescribe the use of any technique as a form of treatment for physical, emotional, or medical problems without the advice of a physician, either directly or indirectly. The intent of the author is only to offer information of a general nature. In the event you use any of the information in this book for yourself, which is your constitutional right, the author and the publisher assume no responsibility for your actions.

Cover image Racing Background © Lkruger | Dreamstime.com
Cover image Racing Border © Mitch1921 | Dreamstime.com

Printed in Australia, UK and USA

DoctorZed Publishing rev. date: 08/04/2024

CONTENTS

Welcome!	vii
A Word of Encouragement	viii
The Winner's Way	ix
Week 1	1
Week 2	11
Week 3	21
Week 4	31
Week 5	41
Week 6	51
Week 7	61
Week 8	71
Week 9	81
Week 10	91
Week 11	101
Week 12	111
Week 13	121
Week 14	131
Week 15	141
Week 16	151
Week 17	161

> Energy flows where your focus goes.

SCOTT ZARCINAS

WELCOME!

Hello and welcome. I'd like to congratulate you on taking this step to unlock the true potential of your life and embark on the process of celebrating your victories.

This journal is an alternative to quick-fix, result-driven recipes for 'success' in life. It is a process of knowing, liking, and trusting yourself better, a process of *how* to celebrate and enjoy life.

And because it is a process it is something that will continue throughout your life. There is no end to the process itself, which may seem contradictory to what the content of this book is about—celebrating the little things and living with greater joy and peace—but what you will find is that the process itself evokes the inherent joy and peace lying at the core of your being that has hitherto been suppressed and dampened by the 'busyness' of our modern lifestyles.

The process, therefore, means constant work on your behalf and to keep persisting with the process of celebrating your wins. As Martin Luther King said: "If not you, then who? If not now, then when?"

It is my hope and intent to now help empower you to the abundance and fullness that life has to offer using the specific knowledge of *The Winner's Way*.

Dr. Scott Zarcinas

A WORD OF ENCOURAGEMENT

This journal is not a magic wand that will make all your problems disappear. Nor is it a magic carpet that will take you to a place far from all your stresses and pains. Rather, this journal will gently remind you that you have the power to find all the joy and happiness you are looking for, no matter what you are going through.

But you are not without help.

This journal will equip you with the necessary tools to master the art of joyous celebration throughout your day. It is designed to be your companion on your journey of personal growth and achievement.

By committing to the regular documentation of your wins, big and small, you will embark on a powerful practice that can significantly transform your experience of life.

As the parable says:

> *Give a man a fish,*
> *You feed him for a day.*
> *Teach a man how to fish,*
> *You feed him for a lifetime.*

THE WINNER'S WAY

THE PRIMARY PURPOSE of this wins journal is to help you acknowledge and celebrate your victories, no matter how small they may seem. In our busy life, it's easy to overlook our accomplishments or brush them aside as insignificant.

The Winner's Way is simply this:

Each success, no matter how minor, contributes to your overall sense of well-being and fulfillment.

By dedicating time each day to reflect on your wins, you're actively shifting your focus towards the positive aspects of your life.

This practice of gratitude and acknowledgment can have profound effects on your mental and emotional well-being, helping you to cultivate a more optimistic outlook and resilience in the face of challenges.

Benefits of Keeping a Wins Journal

1. Increased Gratitude
2. Boosted Self-Belief
3. Motivation and Momentum
4. Reflection and Learning

#1: Increased Gratitude

By starting each day with a focus on gratitude, you'll develop a greater appreciation for the blessings in your life, both big and small. This simple practice can help shift your perspective from what you lack to what you have, promoting a sense of abundance and contentment.

#2: Boosted Self-Belief

Recording your wins allows you to recognise your strengths and accomplishments, boosting your self-belief and confidence.

Over time, you'll build a collection of evidence that proves your capability and resilience, empowering you to tackle future challenges with conviction and self-assuredness.

#3: Motivation and Momentum

Celebrating your wins provides a powerful source of motivation and momentum to keep pushing forward towards your goals.

By acknowledging your progress, you'll feel inspired to continue taking action and striving for excellence in all areas of your life.

#4: Reflection and Learning

This wins journal also serves as a tool for self-reflection and personal growth. By identifying the lessons learned from each day's experiences, you'll gain valuable insights into your strengths, weaknesses, and areas for improvement.

This continuous process of self-discovery is essential for personal development and achieving your full potential.

Approach with an Open Mind

As you embark on this journey with your wins journal, I encourage you to approach it with an open mind and a willingness to embrace new perspectives.

Be kind to yourself and celebrate your successes, no matter how small they may seem. Remember that progress is not always linear, and setbacks are an inevitable part of the journey.

Use your wins journal as a tool for self-compassion and resilience, knowing that each entry brings you one step closer to becoming the best version of yourself.

Commit to the Way

Commit to dedicating time each day to reflect on your wins and express gratitude for the blessings in your life. Trust in the process, and allow yourself to be inspired by your own achievements.

Your wins journal is a testament to your growth, resilience, and unwavering commitment to living a life filled with purpose and joy.

> Build your own dreams or somebody else will hire you to build theirs.

FARAH GRAY

DAILY ENTRY—DATE:

Gratitude:

1.
2.
3.

Wins:

Lessons Learned:

Affirmations:

DAILY ENTRY—DATE:

Gratitude:

1.
2.
3.

Wins:

Lessons Learned:

Affirmations:

DAILY ENTRY—DATE:

GRATITUDE:

1.
2.
3.

WINS:

LESSONS LEARNED:

AFFIRMATIONS:

THE WINNER'S WAY

DAILY ENTRY—DATE:

GRATITUDE:

1.
2.
3.

WINS:

LESSONS LEARNED:

AFFIRMATIONS:

THE WINNER'S WAY

DAILY ENTRY—DATE:

GRATITUDE:

1.

2.

3.

WINS:

LESSONS LEARNED:

AFFIRMATIONS:

DAILY ENTRY—DATE:

Gratitude:

1.

2.

3.

Wins:

Lessons Learned:

Affirmations:

DAILY ENTRY—DATE:

GRATITUDE:

1.
2.
3.

WINS:

LESSONS LEARNED:

AFFIRMATIONS:

Weekly Insights

WEEKLY ENTRY—WEEK ENDING DATE:

Weekly Wins:

Challenges Overcome:

Growth Areas:

Grattitude Recap:

> Every defeat holds the seed of equivalent benefit.

NAPOLEON HILL

DAILY ENTRY—DATE:

GRATITUDE:

1.
2.
3.

WINS:

LESSONS LEARNED:

AFFIRMATIONS:

THE WINNER'S WAY

DAILY ENTRY—DATE:

Gratitude:

1.
2.
3.

Wins:

Lessons Learned:

Affirmations:

THE WINNER'S WAY

DAILY ENTRY—DATE:

Gratitude:

1.
2.
3.

Wins:

Lessons Learned:

Affirmations:

DAILY ENTRY—DATE:

Gratitude:

1.
2.
3.

Wins:

Lessons Learned:

Affirmations:

DAILY ENTRY—DATE:

GRATITUDE:

1.

2.

3.

WINS:

LESSONS LEARNED:

AFFIRMATIONS:

THE WINNER'S WAY

DAILY ENTRY—DATE:

Gratitude:

1.
2.
3.

Wins:

Lessons Learned:

Affirmations:

DAILY ENTRY—DATE:

Gratitude:

1.
2.
3.

Wins:

Lessons Learned:

Affirmations:

Weekly Insights

THE WINNER'S WAY

WEEKLY ENTRY—WEEK ENDING DATE:

Weekly Wins:

Challenges Overcome:

Growth Areas:

Grattitude Recap:

> Gratitude is the single most important ingredient to living a successful and fulfilled life.

JACK CANFIELD

DAILY ENTRY—DATE:

GRATITUDE:

1.
2.
3.

WINS:

LESSONS LEARNED:

AFFIRMATIONS:

DAILY ENTRY—DATE:

Gratitude:

1.
2.
3.

Wins:

Lessons Learned:

Affirmations:

DAILY ENTRY—DATE:

Gratitude:

1.
2.
3.

Wins:

Lessons Learned:

Affirmations:

DAILY ENTRY—DATE:

GRATITUDE:

1.
2.
3.

WINS:

LESSONS LEARNED:

AFFIRMATIONS:

DAILY ENTRY—DATE:

> ## GRATITUDE:
> 1.
> 2.
> 3.

> ## WINS:

> ## LESSONS LEARNED:

> ## AFFIRMATIONS:

DAILY ENTRY—DATE:

Gratitude:

1.
2.
3.

Wins:

Lessons Learned:

Affirmations:

DAILY ENTRY—DATE:

GRATITUDE:

1.
2.
3.

WINS:

LESSONS LEARNED:

AFFIRMATIONS:

Weekly Insights

THE WINNER'S WAY

WEEKLY ENTRY—WEEK ENDING DATE:

Weekly Wins:

Challenges Overcome:

Growth Areas:

Grattitude Recap:

> Look well to this day for it,
> and it alone, is life.

BHAGAVAD GITA

DAILY ENTRY—DATE:

Gratitude:

1.
2.
3.

Wins:

Lessons Learned:

Affirmations:

DAILY ENTRY—DATE:

GRATITUDE:

1.
2.
3.

WINS:

LESSONS LEARNED:

AFFIRMATIONS:

DAILY ENTRY—DATE:

Gratitude:

1.
2.
3.

Wins:

Lessons Learned:

Affirmations:

DAILY ENTRY—DATE:

Gratitude:

1.
2.
3.

Wins:

Lessons Learned:

Affirmations:

DAILY ENTRY—DATE:

GRATITUDE:

1.
2.
3.

WINS:

LESSONS LEARNED:

AFFIRMATIONS:

DAILY ENTRY—DATE:

GRATITUDE:

1.
2.
3.

WINS:

LESSONS LEARNED:

AFFIRMATIONS:

DAILY ENTRY—DATE:

Gratitude:

1.
2.
3.

Wins:

Lessons Learned:

Affirmations:

Weekly Insights

WEEKLY ENTRY—WEEK ENDING DATE:

Weekly Wins:

Challenges Overcome:

Growth Areas:

Grattitude Recap:

"
You either believe miracles
happen every day,
or not at all.
"

ALBERT EINSTEIN

DAILY ENTRY—DATE:

GRATITUDE:

1.
2.
3.

WINS:

LESSONS LEARNED:

AFFIRMATIONS:

DAILY ENTRY—DATE:

GRATITUDE:

1.
2.
3.

WINS:

LESSONS LEARNED:

AFFIRMATIONS:

DAILY ENTRY—DATE:

Gratitude:

1.
2.
3.

Wins:

Lessons Learned:

Affirmations:

DAILY ENTRY—DATE:

GRATITUDE:

1.
2.
3.

WINS:

LESSONS LEARNED:

AFFIRMATIONS:

DAILY ENTRY—DATE:

GRATITUDE:

1.
2.
3.

WINS:

LESSONS LEARNED:

AFFIRMATIONS:

DAILY ENTRY—DATE:

Gratitude:

1.
2.
3.

Wins:

Lessons Learned:

Affirmations:

DAILY ENTRY—DATE:

Gratitude:

1.
2.
3.

Wins:

Lessons Learned:

Affirmations:

Weekly Insights

WEEKLY ENTRY—WEEK ENDING DATE:

Weekly Wins:

Challenges Overcome:

Growth Areas:

Grattitude Recap:

> Growth and increase and life abundant, are the way of nature.

EARL NIGHTINGALE

DAILY ENTRY—DATE:

GRATITUDE:

1.
2.
3.

WINS:

LESSONS LEARNED:

AFFIRMATIONS:

DAILY ENTRY—DATE:

GRATITUDE:

1.
2.
3.

WINS:

LESSONS LEARNED:

AFFIRMATIONS:

DAILY ENTRY—DATE:

GRATITUDE:

1.
2.
3.

WINS:

LESSONS LEARNED:

AFFIRMATIONS:

DAILY ENTRY—DATE:

GRATITUDE:

1.
2.
3.

WINS:

LESSONS LEARNED:

AFFIRMATIONS:

DAILY ENTRY—DATE:

Gratitude:

1.
2.
3.

Wins:

Lessons Learned:

Affirmations:

DAILY ENTRY—DATE:

Gratitude:

1.
2.
3.

Wins:

Lessons Learned:

Affirmations:

DAILY ENTRY—DATE:

Gratitude:

1.
2.
3.

Wins:

Lessons Learned:

Affirmations:

Weekly Insights

THE WINNER'S WAY

WEEKLY ENTRY—WEEK ENDING DATE:

WEEKLY WINS:

CHALLENGES OVERCOME:

GROWTH AREAS:

GRATTITUDE RECAP:

> There are no limits.
> There are only plateaus,
> and you must not stay there,
> you must go beyond them.

BRUCE LEE

DAILY ENTRY—DATE:

GRATITUDE:

1.
2.
3.

WINS:

LESSONS LEARNED:

AFFIRMATIONS:

DAILY ENTRY—DATE:

Gratitude:

1.
2.
3.

Wins:

Lessons Learned:

Affirmations:

THE WINNER'S WAY

DAILY ENTRY—DATE:

Gratitude:

1.
2.
3.

Wins:

Lessons Learned:

Affirmations:

DAILY ENTRY—DATE:

GRATITUDE:

1.
2.
3.

WINS:

LESSONS LEARNED:

AFFIRMATIONS:

DAILY ENTRY—DATE:

GRATITUDE:

1.
2.
3.

WINS:

LESSONS LEARNED:

AFFIRMATIONS:

DAILY ENTRY—DATE:

Gratitude:

1.
2.
3.

Wins:

Lessons Learned:

Affirmations:

DAILY ENTRY—DATE:

Gratitude:

1.
2.
3.

Wins:

Lessons Learned:

Affirmations:

Weekly Insights

THE WINNER'S WAY

WEEKLY ENTRY—WEEK ENDING DATE:

WEEKLY WINS:

CHALLENGES OVERCOME:

GROWTH AREAS:

GRATTITUDE RECAP:

> We can do anything
> we want to if we stick to it
> long enough.

HELEN KELLER

DAILY ENTRY—DATE:

GRATITUDE:

1.
2.
3.

WINS:

LESSONS LEARNED:

AFFIRMATIONS:

DAILY ENTRY—DATE:

GRATITUDE:

1.
2.
3.

WINS:

LESSONS LEARNED:

AFFIRMATIONS:

THE WINNER'S WAY

DAILY ENTRY—DATE:

Gratitude:

1.
2.
3.

Wins:

Lessons Learned:

Affirmations:

DAILY ENTRY—DATE:

Gratitude:

1.
2.
3.

Wins:

Lessons Learned:

Affirmations:

THE WINNER'S WAY

DAILY ENTRY—DATE:

GRATITUDE:

1.
2.
3.

WINS:

LESSONS LEARNED:

AFFIRMATIONS:

THE WINNER'S WAY

DAILY ENTRY—DATE:

Gratitude:

1.
2.
3.

Wins:

Lessons Learned:

Affirmations:

DAILY ENTRY—DATE:

Gratitude:

1.
2.
3.

Wins:

Lessons Learned:

Affirmations:

Weekly Insights

WEEKLY ENTRY—WEEK ENDING DATE:

Weekly Wins:

Challenges Overcome:

Growth Areas:

Grattitude Recap:

> "Do unto others as you would have them do unto you."

THE GOLDEN RULE

DAILY ENTRY—DATE:

GRATITUDE:

1.
2.
3.

WINS:

LESSONS LEARNED:

AFFIRMATIONS:

THE WINNER'S WAY

DAILY ENTRY—DATE:

GRATITUDE:

1.
2.
3.

WINS:

LESSONS LEARNED:

AFFIRMATIONS:

DAILY ENTRY—DATE:

Gratitude:

1.
2.
3.

Wins:

Lessons Learned:

Affirmations:

DAILY ENTRY—DATE:

GRATITUDE:

1.
2.
3.

WINS:

LESSONS LEARNED:

AFFIRMATIONS:

DAILY ENTRY—DATE:

GRATITUDE:

1.
2.
3.

WINS:

LESSONS LEARNED:

AFFIRMATIONS:

THE WINNER'S WAY

DAILY ENTRY—DATE:

GRATITUDE:

1.
2.
3.

WINS:

LESSONS LEARNED:

AFFIRMATIONS:

THE WINNER'S WAY

DAILY ENTRY—DATE:

GRATITUDE:

1.
2.
3.

WINS:

LESSONS LEARNED:

AFFIRMATIONS:

Weekly Insights

WEEKLY ENTRY—WEEK ENDING DATE:

WEEKLY WINS:

CHALLENGES OVERCOME:

GROWTH AREAS:

GRATTITUDE RECAP:

> The two most important days of your life are the day you are born, and the day you find out why.

MARK TWAIN

THE WINNER'S WAY

DAILY ENTRY—DATE:

GRATITUDE:

1.
2.
3.

WINS:

LESSONS LEARNED:

AFFIRMATIONS:

DAILY ENTRY—DATE:

GRATITUDE:

1.
2.
3.

WINS:

LESSONS LEARNED:

AFFIRMATIONS:

THE WINNER'S WAY

DAILY ENTRY—DATE:

Gratitude:

1.
2.
3.

Wins:

Lessons Learned:

Affirmations:

DAILY ENTRY—DATE:

GRATITUDE:

1.
2.
3.

WINS:

LESSONS LEARNED:

AFFIRMATIONS:

THE WINNER'S WAY

DAILY ENTRY—DATE:

Gratitude:

1.
2.
3.

Wins:

Lessons Learned:

Affirmations:

DAILY ENTRY—DATE:

GRATITUDE:

1.
2.
3.

WINS:

LESSONS LEARNED:

AFFIRMATIONS:

DAILY ENTRY—DATE:

Gratitude:

1.
2.
3.

Wins:

Lessons Learned:

Affirmations:

Weekly Insights

THE WINNER'S WAY

WEEKLY ENTRY—WEEK ENDING DATE:

Weekly Wins:

Challenges Overcome:

Growth Areas:

Grattitude Recap:

> "Every single one of us has the power to make and shape our own moments."

HUSEYN RAZA

DAILY ENTRY—DATE:

Gratitude:

1.
2.
3.

Wins:

Lessons Learned:

Affirmations:

DAILY ENTRY—DATE:

GRATITUDE:

1.
2.
3.

WINS:

LESSONS LEARNED:

AFFIRMATIONS:

DAILY ENTRY—DATE:

Gratitude:

1.
2.
3.

Wins:

Lessons Learned:

Affirmations:

DAILY ENTRY—DATE:

Gratitude:

1.
2.
3.

Wins:

Lessons Learned:

Affirmations:

DAILY ENTRY—DATE:

GRATITUDE:

1.
2.
3.

WINS:

LESSONS LEARNED:

AFFIRMATIONS:

DAILY ENTRY—DATE:

GRATITUDE:

1.
2.
3.

WINS:

LESSONS LEARNED:

AFFIRMATIONS:

DAILY ENTRY—DATE:

GRATITUDE:

1.
2.
3.

WINS:

LESSONS LEARNED:

AFFIRMATIONS:

Weekly Insights

WEEKLY ENTRY—WEEK ENDING DATE:

Weekly Wins:

Challenges Overcome:

Growth Areas:

Grattitude Recap:

> Do not seek to change what has come before. Seek to create that which has not.

DAVID AIREY

DAILY ENTRY—DATE:

Gratitude:

1.
2.
3.

Wins:

Lessons Learned:

Affirmations:

DAILY ENTRY—DATE:

GRATITUDE:

1.
2.
3.

WINS:

LESSONS LEARNED:

AFFIRMATIONS:

DAILY ENTRY—DATE:

Gratitude:

1.
2.
3.

Wins:

Lessons Learned:

Affirmations:

DAILY ENTRY—DATE:

GRATITUDE:

1.
2.
3.

WINS:

LESSONS LEARNED:

AFFIRMATIONS:

DAILY ENTRY—DATE:

Gratitude:
1.
2.
3.

Wins:

Lessons Learned:

Affirmations:

DAILY ENTRY—DATE:

GRATITUDE:

1.
2.
3.

WINS:

LESSONS LEARNED:

AFFIRMATIONS:

DAILY ENTRY—DATE:

GRATITUDE:

1.
2.
3.

WINS:

LESSONS LEARNED:

AFFIRMATIONS:

Weekly Insights

THE WINNER'S WAY

WEEKLY ENTRY—WEEK ENDING DATE:

Weekly Wins:

Challenges Overcome:

Growth Areas:

Grattitude Recap:

> "Man is where he is so that he may learn that he may grow."
>
> **JAMES ALLEN**

DAILY ENTRY—DATE:

GRATITUDE:

1.
2.
3.

WINS:

LESSONS LEARNED:

AFFIRMATIONS:

DAILY ENTRY—DATE:

Gratitude:

1.
2.
3.

Wins:

Lessons Learned:

Affirmations:

DAILY ENTRY—DATE:

GRATITUDE:

1.
2.
3.

WINS:

LESSONS LEARNED:

AFFIRMATIONS:

DAILY ENTRY—DATE:

GRATITUDE:

1.
2.
3.

WINS:

LESSONS LEARNED:

AFFIRMATIONS:

DAILY ENTRY—DATE:

GRATITUDE:

1.
2.
3.

WINS:

LESSONS LEARNED:

AFFIRMATIONS:

DAILY ENTRY—DATE:

GRATITUDE:

1.
2.
3.

WINS:

LESSONS LEARNED:

AFFIRMATIONS:

DAILY ENTRY—DATE:

GRATITUDE:

1.
2.
3.

WINS:

LESSONS LEARNED:

AFFIRMATIONS:

Weekly Insights

THE WINNER'S WAY

WEEKLY ENTRY—WEEK ENDING DATE:

WEEKLY WINS:

CHALLENGES OVERCOME:

GROWTH AREAS:

GRATTITUDE RECAP:

> Nothing can bring you peace but yourself. Nothing can bring you peace but the triumph of principles.

RALPH WALDO EMERSON

DAILY ENTRY—DATE:

Gratitude:

1.

2.

3.

Wins:

Lessons Learned:

Affirmations:

DAILY ENTRY—DATE:

GRATITUDE:

1.
2.
3.

WINS:

LESSONS LEARNED:

AFFIRMATIONS:

DAILY ENTRY—DATE:

> ### GRATITUDE:
>
> 1.
> 2.
> 3.

> ### WINS:

> ### LESSONS LEARNED:

> ### AFFIRMATIONS:

DAILY ENTRY—DATE:

GRATITUDE:

1.
2.
3.

WINS:

LESSONS LEARNED:

AFFIRMATIONS:

DAILY ENTRY—DATE:

GRATITUDE:

1.
2.
3.

WINS:

LESSONS LEARNED:

AFFIRMATIONS:

DAILY ENTRY—DATE:

GRATITUDE:

1.
2.
3.

WINS:

LESSONS LEARNED:

AFFIRMATIONS:

DAILY ENTRY—DATE:

GRATITUDE:

1.
2.
3.

WINS:

LESSONS LEARNED:

AFFIRMATIONS:

Weekly Insights

WEEKLY ENTRY—WEEK ENDING DATE:

Weekly Wins:

Challenges Overcome:

Growth Areas:

Grattitude Recap:

> Life isn't about finding yourself. Life is about creating yourself.

GEORGE BERNHARD SHAW

DAILY ENTRY—DATE:

GRATITUDE:

1.
2.
3.

WINS:

LESSONS LEARNED:

AFFIRMATIONS:

DAILY ENTRY—DATE:

Gratitude:

1.
2.
3.

Wins:

Lessons Learned:

Affirmations:

DAILY ENTRY—DATE:

Gratitude:

1.
2.
3.

Wins:

Lessons Learned:

Affirmations:

DAILY ENTRY—DATE:

GRATITUDE:

1.
2.
3.

WINS:

LESSONS LEARNED:

AFFIRMATIONS:

THE WINNER'S WAY

DAILY ENTRY—DATE:

GRATITUDE:

1.
2.
3.

WINS:

LESSONS LEARNED:

AFFIRMATIONS:

DAILY ENTRY—DATE:

Gratitude:

1.
2.
3.

Wins:

Lessons Learned:

Affirmations:

DAILY ENTRY—DATE:

GRATITUDE:

1.
2.
3.

WINS:

LESSONS LEARNED:

AFFIRMATIONS:

Weekly Insights

THE WINNER'S WAY

WEEKLY ENTRY—WEEK ENDING DATE:

WEEKLY WINS:

CHALLENGES OVERCOME:

GROWTH AREAS:

GRATTITUDE RECAP:

> Like scaling a mountain, our dreams are achieved one step at a time, not in large leaps.

SCOTT ZARCINAS

DAILY ENTRY—DATE:

GRATITUDE:

1.
2.
3.

WINS:

LESSONS LEARNED:

AFFIRMATIONS:

DAILY ENTRY—DATE:

GRATITUDE:

1.
2.
3.

WINS:

LESSONS LEARNED:

AFFIRMATIONS:

DAILY ENTRY—DATE:

Gratitude:

1.
2.
3.

Wins:

Lessons Learned:

Affirmations:

DAILY ENTRY—DATE:

GRATITUDE:

1.
2.
3.

WINS:

LESSONS LEARNED:

AFFIRMATIONS:

DAILY ENTRY—DATE:

GRATITUDE:

1.
2.
3.

WINS:

LESSONS LEARNED:

AFFIRMATIONS:

DAILY ENTRY—DATE:

Gratitude:

1.
2.
3.

Wins:

Lessons Learned:

Affirmations:

DAILY ENTRY—DATE:

GRATITUDE:

1.
2.
3.

WINS:

LESSONS LEARNED:

AFFIRMATIONS:

Weekly Insights

THE WINNER'S WAY

WEEKLY ENTRY—WEEK ENDING DATE:

Weekly Wins:

Challenges Overcome:

Growth Areas:

Grattitude Recap:

> If you don't know to which port you are sailing,
> no wind is helpful.

SENECA

DAILY ENTRY—DATE:

Gratitude:

1.
2.
3.

Wins:

Lessons Learned:

Affirmations:

DAILY ENTRY—DATE:

GRATITUDE:

1.
2.
3.

WINS:

LESSONS LEARNED:

AFFIRMATIONS:

DAILY ENTRY—DATE:

Gratitude:

1.
2.
3.

Wins:

Lessons Learned:

Affirmations:

DAILY ENTRY—DATE:

GRATITUDE:

1.
2.
3.

WINS:

LESSONS LEARNED:

AFFIRMATIONS:

DAILY ENTRY—DATE:

Gratitude:

1.
2.
3.

Wins:

Lessons Learned:

Affirmations:

DAILY ENTRY—DATE:

GRATITUDE:

1.
2.
3.

WINS:

LESSONS LEARNED:

AFFIRMATIONS:

DAILY ENTRY—DATE:

GRATITUDE:

1.
2.
3.

WINS:

LESSONS LEARNED:

AFFIRMATIONS:

Weekly Insights

WEEKLY ENTRY—WEEK ENDING DATE:

Weekly Wins:

Challenges Overcome:

Growth Areas:

Grattitude Recap:

> Our attitude towards life determines life's attitude toward us.

EARL NIGHTINGALE

Contractual Agreement:

On this date _____

I _____
do hereby commit to the principles of *The Winner's Way* in order to fulfil my goal of maximising my potential and living a life of happiness, peace, and prosperity.

I recognise that the power to control my experience of life is in my hands and nobody else. I recognise the importance of the process of gratitude and celebrating my victories, no matter how small, and I recognise that this process is a process that never ends.

I hereby make this lifelong commitment to myself.

Signed: _____

OTHER BOOKS BY SCOTT ZARCINAS

Non-fiction

Being YOU!
It's Up to YOU!
The Power of YOU!
The Banana Trap
The Flea Circus

Fiction

Samantha Honeycomb
The Golden Chalice
DeVille's Contract
Ananda
Roadman

Connect with DoctorZed

Facebook: YNSOB.by.Dr.Scott.Zarcinas
LinkedIn: dr-scott-zarcinas-6572399
Instagram: doctorzed_motivational_speaker
Twitter: @DrScottZarcinas
Website: *scottzarcinas.com*

Growing great people is how you grow a great business!

Are you a leader of a team, involved in a team environment, a business owner, or entrepreneur looking to grow your business?

Ask me how I can help your business grow by growing your people.

E: scott.zarcinas@doctorzed.com
W: scottzarcinas.com/contact

The Life You Want, the Way You Want, How You Want!

Looking for a coach or mentor to help you get direction and take your life to the next level?

Ask me how I can help you maximise your capabilities and reach your fullest potential.

E: scott.zarcinas@doctorzed.com
W: scottzarcinas.com/contact

Book DoctorZed for Your Next Function!
Keynotes • MC • Presentations

scottzarcinas.com/book-doctorzed/

www.ingramcontent.com/pod-product-compliance
Lightning Source LLC
LaVergne TN
LVHW010320070426
835507LV00032B/3496